It is with great felicity
I dedicate this book to three
    Delightful, winsome little girls:
Lucretia, Paige, and Betony.

# Of Fairies and Witches and Kisses and Wishes

## Poetry for Children and Adults

### Phoebe Synn

Samuel Earl Simpson
Rosemary Rutland
Trudy Silverheels
Damien Wynter
FXP Carlisle

ARCHER TRENT, PUBLISHER
2017

## Third Edition
ISBN 978-0-9990029-3-3

This is a facsimile edition of the original version produced by Pouty Poppet Press.

A Literary Project of
THE GRIFFOUN SOCIETY
Houston, Texas

# Table of Contents

# Acknowledgment

Twenty years ago I began an international correspondence with a pen pal I had never met face to face and would not meet for fifteen years. Such correspondences are not all that rare, I suppose, but they usually run their course in only a few months. This one, on the other hand, became the basis of a lifetime friendship, the reason being that we shared an interest—nay, an absolute passion—for versifying.

Actually the interest was his; the passion, mine. For him poetry was and is an amusing pastime, but for me it has always been a calling. In any event, when we discovered that we had this occupation in common, we began challenging each other by including in every letter opening lines of a new poem and issuing an invitation to finish the piece. Amazingly, this method worked beautifully for us. Many of the verses in this collection were written in just that fashion.

Only rarely did a challenge go unfulfilled and never for want of trying. In 1995, I think it was, my correspondent sent me the following two lines:

> *From Hooperstown a little rill*
> *Meanders down to Douglasville*

I eventually added three more lines, but I was never fully satisfied with them:

> *And passes on its way a mill,*
> *Where, powered by a waterwheel,*
> *A millstone renders corn to meal.*

I suppose the five lines together are a pretty good

start, but neither he nor I could ever decide where we wanted that poem to go. Over the years I have tried repeatedly to build something new from those two opening lines, but I have never yet done better than I did initially, and I have never got further than one stanza.

Most of our poetry is pretty short, but on one occasion I received in a letter the first stanza for what would almost have to be an epic:

> *A powerful djinni, long trapped in a jug,*
> *To thank me for freeing him, gave me a rug,*
>> *A rug form the Orient magically wrought*
>> *To fly through the air more swiftly than thought.*

Of course, this was an age-old story, and I loved the idea of setting it to verse, but I never could make it work.

Another brief stanza that seemed to have promise but led nowhere went like this:

> *When first I gazed upon the dome*
> *Atop St Peter's Church in Rome,*
>> *My heart was thrilled, and I was filled*
> *With inspiration for this po'm.*

If any reader wishes to take up this challenge, you have my blessing and that of my writing partner to treat these three fragments as your own. I should really like to see what someone else can do with them.

Incidentally, it was my wish that my pen pal, whose nom de plume is *FXP Carlisle*, and I share equally the credit for authorship of this book, but he refused to even consider such an arrangement. He insists upon seeing himself as no more than a facilitator of my literary career, but I know better and do hereby acknowledge the truth of the matter.

I have included three poems he wrote entirely on his own, as well as several more by other authors: Samuel Earl Simpson, Rosemary Rutland, Trudy Silverheels, and Damien Wynter. Each such poem is clearly attributed to its creator. Only those poems not thus attributed are to be understood to be by yours truly.

Indeed, I want to thank everyone who submitted poems for inclusion in this work. In order to remain true to my vision for this title, I was forced to make some difficult choices. All the submissions I received were delightful. I was not disappointed in even one. But some simply did not feel right for this particular collection. It is very likely that at some point in the future, I shall want to use those passed-over poems in another project. I hope the authors will allow it.

*Phoebe Veronica Synn*

# Of Fairies and Witches
## and
## Kisses and Wishes

# Student Witch

Directionless Lucretia Fitch
At last, I hear, has found her niche.
She's studying to be a witch.
        She's bought a cat and pointy hat,
And both of them as black as pitch.

She's mastered spells and learned to fly;
She rides a broomstick through the sky.
She even knows the evil eye.
        But witches' brew
        —that nasty goo—
She's yet to find the nerve to try.

# A Frightful Encounter

If I were to meet a vampire some night,
     I'd ask if he wanted to be my friend.
Well, you never can tell.  A vampire might
     If he didn't already have a friend.
But he'd have to promise me not to bite.


# Protection Against the Black Arts

A potpourri of blue vervain
     And comfrey and trefoil and dill
     With just a pinch of yarrow will
Do service as a witch's bane.

# Dangerous Concoction

So you've the itch to be a witch.
You've learned the Craft and seek the draught
That frees the force that is the source
Of second sight and power of flight.
This recipe was give to me
In 1610 by Goody Gwen.
But, dearie, wait!  The risk is great;
This potent brew could do for you.
My four best friends thus met their ends;
If you survive, you're one in five.
So do beware!  Yet if you dare,
       Boil dragon's blood till thick as mud.
       Add bitter root, an eye of newt,
       A lizard's tail, and stir it well.
Now fill your cup and drink it up.
The twilight zone will be your own,
Unless, instead, you end up dead.

3

## Fanciful Speculation

If fairies were real, then what would they wear?
Diaphanous gowns with stars in their hair?
> Or Tinker Bell costumes?  Or nothing at
> all?
> For where could they shop for fashions so
> small?
If fairies were real, I'll bet they'd go bare.

## Strange Portent

A sign was showed to me today.
It's meaning though I cannot say.
      Out early for my morning jog
      Along the path that skirts the bog,
I found my way by serpents blocked.
Two snakes (in mortal combat locked)
      Writhed fiercely on the narrow trail,
      And each one had the other's tail
Between its teeth.  I had a hunch
That each believed the other lunch.
      Then sure enough, upon my soul,
      Those two snakes ate each other whole.

## In Defense of Werewolves

'Cause werewolves like to act weird and they're
hairy,
    A lot of the time they're misunderstood.
Their growling and howling, I know, seems scary,
    But that's just their way; they really are
    good.

# Garden-Variety Wizard

How Merlin-like to little eyes must he appear, old
Rupert Coors,
Whose hoary mane and leathern face bespeak a
lifetime out of doors!
He mows our lawn and tends the plants and in
between does other chores.
> And wise and fey indeed is he.  His will
> the shrubbery obeys
To form that fairy labyrinth, the leafy, living
corridors
> Of which are hallowed by the bairns.  Wee
> pagans all, they dance his praise;
> His preternatural handiwork they celebrate
> in chants and lays;
> And in their gleeful awe, they hail him
> *Mighty Master of the Maze*.

The Gryphon and the Unicorn

The Gryphon called just yestermorn
Upon his friend the Unicorn
      To ask him what he knew of Man.
      Said he, "I'm led to understand
He's make-believe, and yet I feel,
Within my bones, he might be real."
      "No way!" the Unicorn opined.
      "Consider how a Man's defined;
Then weigh the question logically.
The truth, I think, you'll clearly see."
      And from his lexicon he read,
      "'A creature with a sphinx-like head
And minotaur-like limbs and trunk.'
This myth of Man is purest bunk."
      The Gryphon sighed, "I must agree.
      As odd a beast could never be."

NOTE:  When first I came to Seattle a few years ago, I stayed with friends while searching for a home of my own. Directly above the guest bedroom was the nursery.  Every morning just at sunrise I was awakened by an ungodly clattering caused, I soon learned, by a rocking horse ridden at breakneck speed on the hard-wood floor.  The three-year-old equestrienne, unable to throw her leg over the horse's back while wearing her ankle-length night gown, sensibly dispensed with the inconvenient garment.

## Mistress Godiva

Whilst dew bejewels the countryside,
You mount your little horse with pride.
　　　Then, heedless of propriety,
You take a reckless morning ride.

But if she knew, how horrified
Would be your mommy that you ride
　　　Without a stitch of modesty
And so unladylike astride!

# Desperate Measures

I'm sick and tired of this rejection.
It's time you showed me some affection.
      I'm going to see that voodoo lady
      I've heard about in Little Haiti
And have her whip me up a potion
To guarantee your fond devotion.
      I'll mix it in your mashed potatoes
      Or stir it in your stewed tomatoes.
I'll pour it on your pickled pears,
And then you'll eat it unawares.
      We'll marry, and you'll never know
      What made you start to want me so.

## To Bess

It needn't cause you such distress,
My putting a froggy down your dress
      And pulling on your ponytail.
         How else am I to let you know
      I like you and I think you're  swell?

# Romance in the Round

Bewitched am I by Beverly,
But she loves Bob, who's mad for Bea,
Who has a hopeless crush on Leigh,
      Who's sweet on Eve, who, some believe,
Exhibits signs of liking me.

# My Secret Wish

If wishes really do come true,
As you assure me that they do,
      Then maybe you can tell me why,
      When all my birthday candles I
Extinguished with a single puff,
That snotty Reginald McDuff
      Persists in being so remiss.
      He's yet to steal a single kiss.

# Song of the Gingerbread Baker

Whenever you're craving a yummy treat,
Well, gingerbread girls are ever so sweet.
They're dainty; they're tasty; they're fun to eat.
At one and a quarter, they can't be beat.

# Enunthiation

You know, I uthed to thpeak quite clearly,
But now I lithp and thound tho thilly,
    And all becauthe thith little tooth
    Right here in front ith getting loothe.

## Thief of Hearts

To lovely little Peaches Lasky,
      I gladly did entrust my heart.
      But when, alas, we had to part,
My heart she took to far Alasky.

NOTE: *Billet doux,* usually pronounced billie dew, is a French term meaning love letter.

## Billet Doux

Last night I found a *billet doux*
      Concealed inside the hollow tree.
How breathlessly I read it through!
      With tender words it touchingly
Bespoke undying love and true.
      But then it dawned belatedly
That Paul had written it to Pru.
      Why could it not have been for me
And signed—I blush to say—by you?

i love you.

# Liz McColl

Two things distinguish Liz McColl;
She freckled, and she's very tall.
        But how she wishes she were not!
        She's quite unhappy with her lot.
Her life, it seems, is filled with pain,
She's so convinced that she is plain.
        Yet I, for one, am stuck on Liz;
        I like her just the way she is.
It's elegant to be so tall,
And freckles I love most of all.

## What Is a Freckle?

A freckle is a kissing spot.
At least that's what I'm told by Dot,
And she should know; she has a lot.
    They're on her arms, her nose, her ears.
    It probably would take you years
To kiss each kissing spot on Dot.

# A Teacher's Lament

An absolute pill
Is Madeleine Hill.
She's making me ill;
      She's driving me wild.
      This impudent child
Has a whim of steel.

# In her own Defense

I know my conduct you deplore;
You think me naughty to the core.
      But rules with me do not agree,
And being good is such a bore.

# A Sometimes Slugabed

Today I fain would lie abed
And be a lazy sleepyhead.
     But you can bet, come Saturday,
     I'll rise at dawn to greet the day.
It's getting up for school I dread.

# Metamorphosis
## A True-Life Ugly-Duckling Story

Could you have guessed that Robyn Knox,
     That sweet but gawky little maid
Who used to come to school in frocks
     With hems let down and badly frayed—
Whose toes peeked out from tattered socks—
     Would ever have by seventh grade
Turned into such a total fox?

# Forgetful Me!

Forgetful me! I've left unbuttoned
My shirtsleeves and my collar buttons.
I fear I'll find the only button
Upon my person not unbuttoned
One day will be my belly button.

# Uncertainty
## An Epistemological Dilemma

If I were sure
One could be sure,
I might be sure.
But all that's sure
Is: I'm unsure.

# Hiccups

You know what I think?  I think a—HICCUP—
　　　Is such a rude thing.  It interrupts you
Whenever you're trying to talk—HICCUP—
　　　And makes you make a sound like a
　　　donkey.
I hate when that happens.  Don't you?  HICCUP.

# High Tea

I think it wondrous strange to see
Above the housetops in a tree
A table laid as beautifully
As this one laid by Hillary,
My bestest friend, who graciously
Invited all of us to tea:
My teddy bear, my dolls, and me.

# Lumpy + Bumpy = Grumpy
Trudy Silvereheels

My pillow is lumpy.
My mattress is bumpy.
      I can't get to sleep.
      And when I don't sleep,
The next day I'm grumpy.

# Dreams

Some dreams you cherish, and some you regret.
Some you remember, and some you forget.
Some dreams are happy, and some dreams are sad.
Nightmares are dreams that are scary and bad.
Dreams make your blush or else giggle or cry.
Dreams: we all have them, but no one knows why.

# Slumber Party

At Amy's all-night, Meghan Taft
Wore jammies with a window aft
And wondered why her friends all laughed.
How could she not have been aware
Her flap was down, her bottom bare?
You'd think she would have felt a draft.

# Rocket Ace

As nap time overtakes our Tracy,
Sleepy little rocket ace,
She drifts away to outer space.
She'll visit Mars and distant stars
With greetings from the human race.

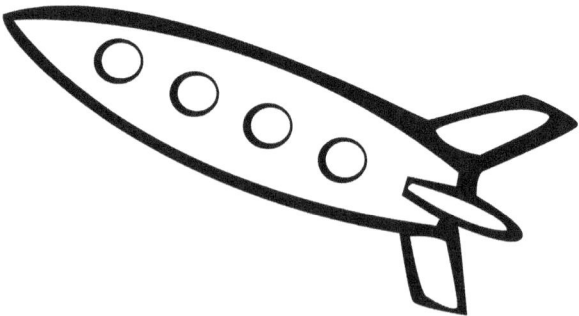

# My Secret Playmate

When no one else has time for me,
I still can count on Emily.
      She thinks I'm nice and tells me so.
      She follows everywhere I go,
And anything I want to do
She says is what she wants to too.
      We never bicker, never fight.
      She even sleeps with me at night.

My parents don't believe she's real.
Imagine how that makes her feel.
      But who can blame them?  Emily
      Will show herself to only me.
She hides when grown-ups come around,
And like a mouse, makes not a sound.
      She waits until they go away
      And then comes out again to play.

# Sweet Temptation

Oh, tempt me not with chocolate mousse
Or crème brulée or charlotte russe.
      If I but dream, as I do now,
      About dessert—don't ask me how—
It shows up on the old caboose.

# El Sid
## A Tribute Composed in a Sushi Restaurant

I'll bet there's not another kid
In second grade as brave as Sid.
Would you have done what he just did?
Would you have dared to eat a squid?

# Brooke's Nook

A little hidey hole has Brooke
Beneath the stair, a secret nook,
Where no one ever thinks to look,
      A place of her own to be alone
And curl up with her favorite book.

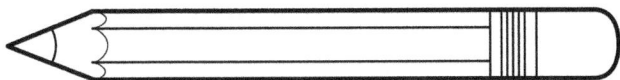

# A Missive Anxiously Awaited

A missive anxiously awaited
Arrived today all decorated
  With flowers, butterflies, and hearts.
  "Dear Fee-Bee, how are you?" it starts.
It's from my little pen pal Blaire.
I'd know that printing anywhere.
  Her upright letters, straight and neat,
  Like soldiers, march across the sheet
The latest goings-on to tell.
She's had the flu, but now she's well.
  And someone by the name of *Mittens*
  Just blest her with a bunch of kittens.
She helps her mother like she should.
Her marks in school are very good.
  In art she's painting me a horse,
  A black Arabian of course.
She's sad that I'm so far away;
She thinks about me every day.
  The fun we shared she says she misses,
  Then closes with a line of kisses.

NOTE: Skones are very like buttermilk biscuits, except that they are sweet and often have dried fruit mixed into the dough. In Scotland, where I lived as a child, skones are pronounced as though spelled s-k-o-o-n-s, to rhyme with spoons. In England and in America, of course, most people pronounce the word to rhyme with stones, but that will not work in this poem, which after all is about life in a Scotish castle.

# The Bubble-Bath Club

The five wee lassies of Calendar Hall,
Patrice and Paige, Denise, Danielle, and Moll,
      This summer established a bubble-bath
      club,
      Which nightly convenes in the nursery tub
As soon as their supper and pudding are done.
But ere they get 'round to the business of fun,
      Their elbows and knees they dutifully
      scrub.
      They're packed like sardines in that claw-
      foot tub
With rose-scented bubbles up to their chins.
And now the merriment truly begins
      As tub toys they add to their  cannibal stew.
      They soak and they play until Nanny
      McGroo

Entices them out with the promise of scones.
Their fingers and toes are as wrinkled as prunes.
> With giggling and shoving, they pat
> themselves dry,
> And then for their treat to the kitchen they
> hie
In slippers and gowns that Nanny laid out.
They're full of contentment, I haven't a doubt,
> When their mummies come up to kiss them
> goodnight,
> To tuck them all in, and to turn out the
> light.

## Life's not Fair

It's clear to me that life's not fair,
Else I'd have straight, not curly, hair,
> And also I could stay up late
> And never eat the foods I hate.
If life were fair, my dog would do
The tricks I've tried to teach him to,
> A certain little girl I know
> Would beg to have me for her beau,
I'd never have to study math,
Do boring chores, or take a bath.
> Nor would I ever have to wear
> A suit and tie if life were fair.

## The Big Parade

At first you only hear the drums,
But then the sound of bagpipes comes,
     And though you cannot see her yet,
     You know a leggy majorette
With tasseled boots will soon come prancing
Behind the color guard advancing,
     And she'll be followed by the band—
     And they'll be playing something grand—
Then mummers, jugglers, mimes and clowns,
And pretty girls in pretty gowns,
     Perhaps the local fire brigade.
     It's going to be a great parade!

A company of fusiliers
At such occasions oft appears,
  And Mounties dressed in scarlet coats.
  There ought to be a zillion floats.
Politicos and movie stars
Will wave at you from open cars.
  The saddle club should be the last
  When floats and marchers all have passed.
You'll want to be where you can see
What truly promises to be
  The best parade that's ever been.
  But when's it ever to begin?

## Babs and Colette at the Beach

FXP Carlisle

Of all the lovely things to do
In summer under skies of blue,
  The best, Colette and Babs agree,
Are done on weekends by the sea:

Like strolling on a lonely strand
And finding footprints in the sand,
  Like catching sight of distant sails,
Or better yet, of breaching whales.

They love the sand, the salty air,
The noisy seagulls everywhere.
  They love to smell the oceany smells
  And hear the clanging buoy bells.

And at the beach they get to eat
Most every kind of seafood treat:
      Pink little shrimps in cups of ice
      And mussels served on beds of rice,

New England chowder, rolls and slaw,
And oysters on the half shell raw,
      Fillets of flounder, stuffed and broiled,
      And langostinos freshly boiled.

The early hours are best to swim,
And Mommy always goes with them.
      With fins and goggles they explore
      The wonders of the ocean floor.

They build a castle with a moat
In which to sail a tiny boat.
      They pick up scallops from the bay
      And watch some porpoises at play.

But as the morning sun climbs higher,
The little girls begin to tire.
      When Mommy says it's time to go,
      They trudge back to their bungalow.

And there, so not to track inside
The tar that's washed up by the tide,
      The bottoms of their feet they clean
      With stuff that smells like gasoline.

They shower and their hair they rinse.
Their suits they hang across a fence,
       Then scamper fast indoors to dry
       Before they're seen by passersby.

For lunch they dress in matching frocks
And in some restaurant near the docks
       Discuss what other kinds of fun
       They'll have before their weekend's done.

They'll comb the beach for pretty shells
To bring home in their little pails.
       And in the surf they'll splash and wade
       With Mommy watching from the shade.

Their frocks, of course, will end up wet,
But Mommy never seems to fret.
       She knows they'll dry out in the sun
       As up and down the beach they run.

Then by and by in Mommy's lap
Colette will lay her head to nap.
       And whilst she sleeps, her sister Babs
       May try her luck at netting crabs.

And later on the beach at night
They'll build a fire for heat and light
       And cook their supper out of doors
       And for dessert make chocolate s'mores.

And when Colette and Babs are grown
And each has children of her own,
> The memories they'll cherish most
> Will be of weekends at the coast.

# How to Write a Poem

The difficult part is how you will start.
But once you've begun, keep on till you're done.
Of course, you should plan as well as you can.
You have to decide how long and how wide
Your poem will be.  That's really the key.
Now what will you say?  And what's the best
        way?
On this you should trust me: meter's a must.
And don't waste your time on verse without
        rhyme.
As hard to begin is how you will end.
And when you have met this challenge, there's yet
One other small chore you dare not ignore.
You still have to pick—and this is the trick—
A title that's right, not pompous or trite.
So now you're all through; there's no more to do.
Your poem, I'm glad to say, is not bad.

# Poet's Apology

My verses are dumb;
    I know that they're dumb.
        But they're not so dumb,
            I protest, as some.

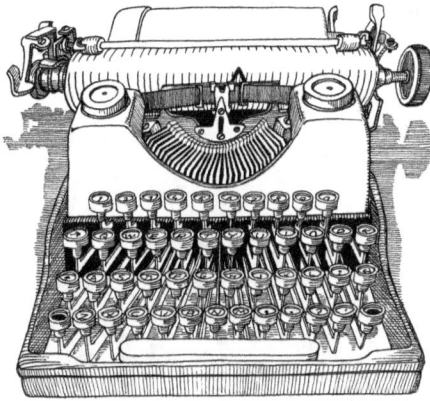

# On Writer's Block
## An Ultimatum

I can't ignore and won't excuse
The wicked way that you abuse
    Me.  Treat me square or—this I swear—
I'll find myself another muse.

# Van Who?

Poor Vincent's work is very dear.
They say he sacrificed an ear
  For someone who refused his heart.
  His suffering sanctified his art
And likewise guaranteed his fame.
But how should one pronounce his name?
  Some say "Van Goff."  Some say "Van
  Go."
  But I'm not Dutch, nor claim to know.

# Weird

The weirdest kid I've ever known
Is Emerson Nathaniel Sloan.
   He puts his coat on wrong side out
   And leaves his shirttail hanging out.
He always seems about to lose
His beltless pants.  He wears his shoes
   In unmatched pairs and likes to munch
   On chocolate-covered ants for lunch.

# An Unpleasant Reminder

I'd never say, "I told you so."
I simply wouldn't stoop so low.
I'm too discreet for that; although
Were I to tell the truth, you know,
I really did. I told you so.

# Child of the Streets
### Trudy Silverheels

In Guatemala, living wild,
An orphaned or abandoned child
    From violence is never safe.
    And every hungry little waif,
Who begs or steals the scraps she eats,
With thousands like herself competes.
    She's likely never known a bed,
    But in the gutter lays her head,
Else huddles in some alleyway.
Nor does she carefree run and play.
    On childish things she has no claim;
    Survival is her only game.

# Martial Mice

Rosemary Rutland

Last night when I was safe in bed
      And supposed to be asleep,
I heard the finest music
      And thunderous marching feet.

At first I covered up my head
      And played I didn't hear,
But then I knew I had to know
      What feet were drawing near.

There was a great parade of mice.
      They came by twos and fours.
They marched along the baseboards.
      They poured in all the doors.

Those wandering rodents marched and sang
      A military air.
There soon were nine of them abreast
      To mount the third-floor stair.

I dared not follow such a band,
      But I know they were a sight,
For they climbed out on the rooftop
      And marched and sang all night.

# Blocks
Rosemary Rutland

I like blocks to build a castle.
    I like blocks to stack and haul.
I like blocks to make a mountain.
    And I love to see them fall.

# Me
Rosemary Rutland

A grain of sand can't be a snail
    No matter how it tries.
A frog can't simply rig a sail
    And be a thing that flies.

A dog will never be a cat
    If it meows a year.
A ball will never be a bat.
    It couldn't happen here.

A butterfly can't be a flea.
    A violet can't be a tree.
A cruising fly can't be a bee.
    And only I can be a me.

# Words
Rosemary Rutland

A book is a first-rate attraction,
   With pictures and stories and such,
But the words in a book are important,
   Since pictures can fool you so much.

The words have definite meanings,
   Exact and unchanging as stone.
To keep them, you use them as much as you like
   To get things or talk on the phone.

Some words are funny, like *fungus*.
   Some words are sad, like *good-bye*.
Some words are bandits, like *knowledge*
   Or *gnat* or *gnome* or *sigh*.

# Why Must You Always Disagree?

Why must you always disagree?
Do you just like to needle me?
   If I say "yes," then you say "no."
   If I say "come," then you say "go."
Why must you always disagree?

## Sabrina on Safari

*Sabrina*'s my name.
Exploring's my game.
   Safaris have earned
Me fortune and fame.

My exploits are known
In darkest Gabón,
   Djibouti, and even
Sierra Leone.

I've sailed all the seas
From Crete to Belize,
   Antarctica to
The Florida Keys.

I've crossed the Sudan
With a caravan
   And carved out a trail
Through the Yucatan.

I've even been seen
To picnic between
    A witch doctor and
A cannibal queen.

And once for a zoo
I captured a gnu
    And also a chimp
And a zebra too.

I've charted Rangoon,
Explored Cameroon,
    And given the chance,
I'd visit the moon.

The snowy Ukrain
I've seen from a train.
    To Moscow and Minsk
I've flown on a plane.
I'm fluent in French.
(Berlitz is a cinch.)
    The Spanish I know
Will do in a pinch.

Adventures I've had
In places like Tchad,
    Where insects and snakes
Are miserably bad.

From primitive rites
To the northern lights,
    I've witnessed a heap
Of marvelous sights.

Yet, while I may roam
To Lisbon and Nome,
　　　The place I like best
Is still my own home.

# I Should Have Been an Eskimo

I should have been an Eskimo,
For living in a house of snow,
      I think, would be especially nice,
      And going fishing through the ice
Would likewise be a lot of fun.
I'd play beneath the midnight sun,
      And on the frozen waste I'd sled.
      I'd never go to school.  Instead,
I'd hunt the fiercest polar bear
To turn him into clothes to wear.
      It's what the Eskimos all do.
      I'm sure that I could do it too.

# Mother Nature
### Damien Wynter

Though Mother Nature's seldom kind,
Her interest must we ever mind.
      Her preservation serves us well.
      Extinction threatens if we fail.
Her fate and ours are intertwined.

# What's on the Menu?

Were you an owl, you'd dine on nice,
Delicious lizards, scrumptious mice,
    And for dessert a snake or two,
    'Cause that's what owls are s'posed to do.
You'd eat them raw, not even hot.
Be glad an owl is what you're not.

## Creepy Crawlies

Why do there have to be spiders and snakes?
I wonder if maybe there not mistakes,
Such as God, supposedly, never makes.

# Carrie
### FXP Carlisle

So sweetly beguiling and spritely is Carrie,
So puckishly playful and mirthful and merry,
She must, as a babe, have been kissed by a fairy.

## Welcome to a new Arrival
### FXP Carlisle

Ciara Katherine, pink and new,
How joyfully we welcome you!
      We pledge to ever do our best
      To see your life be richly blest
With all that's lovely, good, and true.

# Pearl

Although be searched the whole wide world,
A more enchanting little girl,
Could not be found, methinks, than Pearl.

## Heather Chase

Amongst the charms of Heather Chase,
I count the sweetness of her face,
  Her twinkling eyes, her open smile
  (So innocent of any wile),
Her disposition, and her grace.

# What to Do?

My plans for today were to hang out with Faye,
        But Faye has the flu. So what shall I do?
The new girl next door asked me to the shore,
        But I couldn't go; my mommy said no.
I'd like to play jacks with Marsha and Max,
        But they're at the mall; they're shopping
        for fall.
And Kimberly Krause, who loves to play house,
        Has gone to the gym to jog and to swim.
With Heidi and Hope I used to jump rope,
        But they've moved away, I'm sorry to say.
And Pammy and Patty are out with their daddy.
        The Tomlinson twins don't want to be
        friends,
And Stacy's still mad I mentioned to Chad
        What she said to Lee, who told it to me.
Patricia can't play; she's grounded today.
        And Judith and Jo have gone to a show.
At Children's Museum are Carolyn Kim
        And Muffie McPhee. They might have
        asked me!
Miranda McBride has gone for a ride,
        And Bambi and Blair have lambs in the
        fair.
No need to ask Tammy or Sarah or Sammy;
        They're taking their pet to visit the vet.
And Rita Del Rey, who lives down the way,
        Is practicing dance with Harriet Hance.
Fiona and Freddie are just getting ready
        To go on a plane to see their Aunt Jane.

There's no one about; my friends are all out
        Or busy or ill.  How lonely I feel!
Delilah and Dawn are mowing their lawn,
        And Natalie Newell is draining her pool.
Delicia and Devon and Brenda and Bevin
        Are all at the zoo, and Tiffany too.
Penelope Proctor has gone to the doctor.
        She's come down with spots and has to get
        shots.
Belinda and Bart are studying art,
        And Hildegard Hughes is away on a cruise.
The Brownies have taken, unless I'm mistaken,
        An overnight hike to Sweetwater Dike.
In macramé class are Kevin and Cass,
        And Kitty and Kate are learning to skate.
To see what was new I telephoned Dru,
        But Dru wasn't home; she's visiting Rome.
So then I called Claire, and she wasn't there;
        She'd gone to the lake with Becky and
        Blake.
But Claire's sister Sue said I should call you.
        So what do you say?  Would you like to
        play?

# My Dog Charlie

Samuel Earl Simpson

The very doggiest kind of dog
Is my dog Charlie.
You'll never see him catching fish
Or riding on a Harley.

He never plays computer games,
He never paints his house
You'll never see him read a poem
Or argue with his spouse.

There's lots of things he doesn't do
Which is the way with dogs,
A sort of bond he shares with other
Creatures such as frogs.

And yet to bark at people
Riding by on bikes
Is one of the important things
That Charlie really likes.

And he must dig his trenches
All around the yard,
For he was meant for catching moles
And catching moles is hard.

I look with admiration
On one of Heaven's least,
Faithful, though uncertain
When bowing, which is east.

## I Want a Pet

I want a pet, but not a rat
And not a lizard or a bat.
My weirdo brother has a rat.
He thinks that yucky things like that
Make perfect pets, but I prefer
A cuddly pet with fluffy fur:
Perhaps a playful pussy cat.
And when I pat it, it'll purr.

## Mistress of Disguise

You probably think I'm one of the guys.
But I'm not.  I'm a girl.  I'm in disguise.
      In Daddy's old clothes with a mustache
      and nose,
I'm hot on the trail of enemy spies.

## Green with Admiration

I do so envy Rosie Klein,
Who's blest with hair that's baby-fine
And dimples that I wish were mine.
      I'd love to have her charm, her style,
      Her big blue eyes, her perfect smile,
And most of all, her cute behind.

# Who's Who

A headless highwayman is Mitch,
And Wanda is a wicked witch.
      A little imp is Imogene,
      But just tonight.  It's Halloween!

A creepy, greenish ghoul is Brent,
And Jacquey is a jack-o-lent.
      A scary skeleton is Skeet,
      And I'm a goblin.  Trick or treat!

# Freebooter

Whose eyes are those (or dare I ask)
That laugh behind a pirate's mask?
      This dread corsair with corn-silk hair
Can only be Priscilla Trask.

# Two Riddles in Rhyme

## What Am I Thinking of?

I'm thinking of a bug so wee
He's really very hard to see.
Oh, much, much smaller than a bee.
  No, not a chigger, not a louse.
It has to rhyme.  Of course, a flea.

## Who Am I?

I was a tadpole and I swum
  In the goldfish pond till legs I growed.
  This gutter spout's my new abode,
And here I wait for bugs to come,
Which end up in my tummy-tum.
  By now you've guessed that I'm a toad.

# L' Envoi

Dear Reader,
     For now we've come to the end.
In hopes you've enjoyed my rhymes, I extend
An invite to write and your picture to send.
Time reading and answering letters you've penned
Are the hours that I most pleasantly spend.
Remember me always and count me your friend.

     Sincerely,

*Phoebe Veronica Synn*

# About the Contributors
to this Work

# Samuel Earl Simpson

Samuel Earl Simpson picked cotton and went fishing with his grandfather. He always watches for the new moon. He cannot decide between April and October. But then why should he? He will never again visit Paris in August.

# FXP Carlisle

FXP Carlisle was born on the move and has remained a gypsy all his life. He is a printmaker by vocation; a writer by avocation.

# Damien Wynter

Damien Wynter, originally from Prescott, Arizona, resides now in the Texas Hill Country, where he teaches basic composition and creative writing. His home, a modest two-room cabin overlooking the Guadalupe River, is facetiously called the *Wynter Palace*.

# Rosemary Rutland

Rosemary Rutland, a native Texan, spent a lot of years traveling the the world with her military husband Don. She reared four children and helped out with a bunch of grand-children, for whom she wrote poetry. She holds strong beliefs in house plants, full cookie jars, homemade chili sauce, and rocking chairs. The Rutlands, married for seventy-one years, now live in Florida.

# Trudy Silverheels

Trudy Lynn (Bootsy) Silverheels was born in rural Yavapai County, Arizon. Most of her early child-hood was spent there and in Albuquerque, New Mexico. At age twelve she accompanied her family on a two-week vacation to Mexico. That vacation turned into a permanent relocation. Four years later she graduated high school in Coyoacán. After earning a degree from Mexico's National Autonomous University, she returned to the United States for graduate studies, upon comple-tion of which she embarked upon an extended tour of Europe, Asia, and South America. Today she makes her home in Houston, Texas.